THE FAT-HEN
FIELD HOSPITAL
Poems 1985–1992

OTHER WORKS BY CATHERINE BYRON

Settlements (Taxus, 1985)

Samhain (Taxus/Aril, 1987)

Out of Step:
Pursuing Seamus Heaney to Purgatory
(Loxwood Stoneleigh, 1992)

Settlements & Samhain
(Loxwood Stoneleigh, 1993)

THE FAT-HEN
FIELD HOSPITAL
Poems 1985–1992

by Catherine Byron

LOXWOOD STONELEIGH

BRISTOL

First published by Loxwood Stoneleigh in 1993, with financial assistance
from East Midlands Arts

Copyright © 1993 Catherine Byron

Designed and typeset by Falling Wall Press Ltd, Bristol
Printed and bound in Great Britain by BPCC Wheatons Ltd, Exeter
Cover printed by Doveton Press Ltd, Bristol

Front cover: 'Fat Hen' by Emma Byron
Back cover: 'Fat-Hen' by Catherine Byron

British Library Cataloguing-in-Publication Data
A catalogue record for this book is available from the British Library.

ISBN 1 85135 20 9
Loxwood Stoneleigh
11 Colston Yard, Colston Street, Bristol BS1 5BD, England

Contents

/over

Acknowledgements

Poems in this book have previously been published in *Anglo-Welsh Review*, *The Countryman*, *Critical Survey*, *Folded Sheets*, *Giant Steps*, *The Green Book*, *Honest Ulsterman*, *Lines Review*, *Malahat Review*, *The Marlburian*, *New Poetry from Oxford*, *The North*, *Poetry Ireland Review*, *Poetry Review*, *Prospice*, *The Rialto*, *Sunk Island Review* and *Writing Women*. 'This Was *Halal*' was a major prizewinner in the 1992 National Poetry Competition.

I

THE FAT-HEN FIELD HOSPITAL

Lady Day

It is the hungry gap.
Worn teeth scrape
at kale stems' marrow.
Neaps are dry.

Hedgebottoms brighten
with useless green –
herbrobert, goosegrass
in their waiting rings.

We trench potatoes
in the warming earth,
broadcast dredge corn
on a clammy acre.

Weeks of no movement
on the surface soil.
Harvest is months away.
Stock is starved.

Getting Tough

For the first killing we left you there alone
my aunt and I. Took the children to some fair
that celebrated farming's age of steam.
Thrashing machines, steam tractors. That sort of thing.
The billy kid you stunned, or tried to stun
with the six-pound mallet, was *very hard to kill.*
I didn't really know what I was doing
but once I'd started, knew I couldn't stop.
I think he was conscious when I cut his throat.

It was 'culling' with the laying hens.
After the first try, when you wrung a neck
so well the head unscrewed, you thought you'd use
the six-pound mallet for the hens as well.
I held their heads down on the chopping block
by the back shed door. You tried to aim
the hammer smartly. Sometimes you half-missed.

But for the cock who terrorised the children
we read up first on how to kill a goose:
broom handle over the neck, one's feet astride,
and then a neat jerk upwards with its body.
It took the two of us, and didn't work
the first time. Fourth, I think. Mallet again.

My love, how did we get this far stepped in?
You never had a hammer in your hand
until you married me. Manual tools
the mark of manual work, your father said,
and hid all his in a roll of blackened oilcloth
down with the coal. You a white-collar boy.

Now you are out all hours, stretching barbed wire
between fencing posts, hammering stobs in
with the twelve-pound fencing mallet. The six-pounder
you keep for work that's close to home, jobs
that I can witness, be the helpmeet to.

The Disbudding Iron

To my daughters, who were five and three

She was the tiny chestnut of a pair
this nanny kid, her bully brother
haunched at birth for mounting.
He grew horns. But she
to be a good herd-sister must
not head up so.

I held her tight, her week-old bundle of sticks
pulsing her pint of blood in rapid fear.
'There are no nerves,' he said,
'not here on the skull's hard top.'
On the flame-set iron the colours ran with heat.
He soldered then in the longest moment
those horn-buds to her brain,
welded sprout to root.

You two, shut out for the act,
smelled the pain in the branding stench.
And we joked, didn't we,
when you saw as you had to
those huge raw circles on her brow:
'Sanda has snails, red snails on her head.
Sanda's a snail-goat now.'

The Favour

We made a cattle-crush. Barred the stile,
swung the field gate round at an awkward angle.
Our usual make-do.
Inveigled the four calves in
with food, then failing that, fear.
I fastened the hurdle and stood
aside, my part in this over.

It was just you and him from then.
Jim? Doug? A friend of a friend. He knelt
to the first skinny scouring snivelling calf
and made a cut with a knife at the top of its scrotum.
He put his upturned face into it then
getting right down and nuzzling up like a suckler.
Found his mouthful quickly, and clamped on it.

When he came out from under
it was as though the man were pulling dough
just for that second. White
glistening strings stretched
from his mouth to its belly.
For the next second
man and calf held a harp
in the air between them.
His teeth were the pegs
and its belly the sounding board
for the wind-moaning it made.
Then ligaments plucked free,
sprang back from each to each
and the calf cried out in its throat.
The man spat a marbled egg into the dirt,
and picked at his teeth.
Hawked and spat again.
Between the calf's back legs
a couple of strands still hung
like a thin umbilicus.

I was way away
in the screen of the alders.
It was you who held those calves
one at a time while that man
went down on them. You
who grabbed the next.
He who kicked each pair
of steamy testicles clear
for the watching dog.
It was you and the man and the dog
and the four bull calves
all hurdled there by the gate
for that intimate act.

Fat-Hen

You ask me to plough the ground: shall I
take a knife and tear my mother's bosom?
You ask me to cut grass and make hay and
sell it and be rich like white men; but how
dare I cut my mother's hair?

Smohalla, a 19th century Native American

Today, when I went out to garden, the bare soil
of my small clearing distressed me. That earth is distressed.
I have scraped it, and shaken it by the shoulders: 'What!
letting in goosegrass again?' I've warned it – how
many times? – not to cradle weeds. It doesn't learn.

Our daughter, even at ten
would follow me in the furrows to pick up the wounded,
her field hospital a row of plastic pots
where they lingered, astonished exotics:

Chickweed.   Dandelion.   Horsetail.

For years since I've persisted in wringing their necks
in the abattoir of my weeding, taken a blade
that is not the blade of harvest, and run them through.
Weeds fall with no sound or struggle. Not
like the old layer whose head came off in your hand.
She staggered about the yard over and over
dragging her whites in the jugular spangles of red.

Today, I walked back to the house that you have left
between grasses I have long since ceased to mow
and I wished I could sweep like a Buddhist the path before me
lest my feet in falling should crush
                              any creature,
any creature.

This Was Halal

in a stone-built shed in Scotland
when the man with a licence to slaughter
lifted the five-month billy, all four hobbled limbs
and the asymmetrical ruminant body of him
into the metal wheelbarrow, so that his head
hung over the rod-rolled edge.
No ceremony of self-importance, just a quick
and single stroke with a blade.
And so he unlaced the carotid, and its small spurt, spurt
was what I caught, not entirely, in the
plastic bowl that I still have used, years since.
It was only afterwards that I asked 'So
no stunning, then?' 'I have to at work,' he said
'but I love to slaughter in peace, in a place like this
away from the smell of a thousand other deaths.'
Just the bleat of the kid, and of his brother outside
that had no inkling yet it was his turn next in the barrow.
'Look,' he said, holding his hands in the air,
'honest, I left the gun behind today. Won't tell, will you?'
Together we hauled the billy so that the last
fluids drained from its wound, and then he opened
another – the abdomen, sex to sternum. The packed case spilled
its ruffled whites and ambers and reds
into a bucket. I could make out the lights
as he wrenched them free. The liver. The heart.
'Ever want a job?' he asked as I finished
a quick swab down of the floor, of the splattered barrow.
I covered over the bowl and the bucket with empty plastic sacks.
There was no concealing the carcase.
'A job? Shall I fetch his brother?'
'Aye, we're as ready as can be.
Ever need a job, though, call me at the abattoir.
I pay good money to women. There's not many
has a call for it. Them that do
have a feel. They're the best gut-men I know.'

By Ampney Crucis

The day you decided to walk out of our lives
or rather to drive out, and call back later
with a Transit van for your things,
the day you walked over a stone bridge
and down to a rivermeadow with me beside you
one flesh still, but only for about
two hundred or so more hours

it was really the ghost of your father
you were taking by the elbow
your father with that fluid about his heart
his chest cavity filling, filling
and the doctors drawing it off hopelessly
with great hollow needles,
your father calling for plums in late November
twenty years before
when out-of-season fruit was still a wonder
and you'd found some, round and crimson from California
down in the city market after school –

and that evening he had been too ill to know,
his heart and the cavity round his heart
too full now for plums, even the idea of plums.

You were walking with me under the willows near Ampney, but I
was already gone from your knowing,
I the samaritan listener to whom you repeated
I never knew my father as a man myself,
I was only sixteen, on the verge of it
but I never knew him except as a child,
I never knew my father.

We sat down side by side on the bank of that river
and now I was sure. You'd leave us,
move in with your lover. Our daughters
on the verge of the verge of becoming
women would lose their father.

Perhaps one day they would know you,
at eighteen, or twenty-eight. Grown up anyway.
You might not, like him, be dead.

Slug

She dealt with the swarm of flying ants
with hairspray she said.
It was what was to hand.
Her bathroom was full of them *and*
they had wings WINGS
can you imagine? she said.
My recoil was from her.
I couldn't do it, I thought
to wings or slime or whatever.

I had slugs in mind
all the ones I'd gently shooed
from my eggshell-ramparted seedlings
in the springs I'd had seedlings.
No copper stuff or capital punishment,
no traps of beer.

I'd offered the tender shoots in expiation
and for the repose of the soul
of that green and apricot slug –
the one in our tent at the edge of Heythrop Wood
in the first year of our marriage.
It had snugly socketed into the toe
of my gumboot overnight. Unknowing
I rammed and rammed it, thick socks and all
in the morning. Tight fit too tight.
Sockwool claggy with mash when I withdrew
to see what was there.

But recently when it came to another swarmtime
I acted just like my friend
with the same positive witting slaughter.
Under my heel, I suppose, underfoot anyway
our marriage got crushed with a tiny creak like a cinder
the moment I stepped from the ring of my things
to the dracula smile of my lover.
He was what was to hand.

Home Visit

When the doctor came and stood by her bed
asking *how much blood, exactly,*
she had no words –
could only pull back the sheet
and the pink cellular blankets
and show him the scarlet stain
that was pooling now, too fast
for the mattress to drink it
so that the blood rippled a little
in a lake between her thighs
and her nightdress was sticky with it
right across.

Why on earth not call me sooner?
but his voice switched over to calmness
or rather to calming, as he spoke of
what must be done, and packed her
with fresh towels, three, four,
that were slipping already now
as he talked her through,
raising her feet on pillows
just till the ambulance came.

And still she could say no word.
Only as he pulled the covers
back over, and the great marrowbone
rolled out from a fold in the rug,
a knuckle all chewed and hollow,
the tendon strings licked grey
and matted with fibres, only then
did she stumble out: *Dog's.*
She could sense his recoil
greater than from her bleeding.

For days now the bone had been lapped
in the rug, for the dog to re-find
each time he jumped to be with her.
And each day as the bleeding grew
from that first brown show to the
scarlet and pain of yesterday, all through
the hours of unnamed contractions
that knuckle had been a weight
she could count on, holding her down.

And now it was counterweight
to the soft unboned unskinned
motion she'd passed as she'd clutched
the side of the bed, astride the bucket,
the lump small as a sparrow,
with hands and eyes and sex.
Quite dead in a pool of bloody water
in the splashed enamel bucket.

She wanted the marrowbone to be there
on the bed always, pinning the clothes,
smelling of flesh's inwardness
and specially while she was to be carted
elsewhere, put under, and the
last tissues that had been between them
scraped from her emptiness, dumped.
She lay, at home still for these few
last moments, hardly hearing the suck of tyres
on the wet street, the opening of doors.

She was seeing her child swim down
the drains and sewers hours before
from when she'd pulled the chain.

Disappearance

When I was mirror to you
and my silvering
reflected too much, foxed,
you conjured another
looking-glass woman
just to your right of my face.

Good. Now I didn't exist
I could slip from beside your gaze.
I walked out soon after
with a bag of light night things.
I had an appointment that death,
I hoped, would cut in on.

It was June. Larkspur
and salvia in the formal gardens
saluted me as I walked
alone through the city.
It was only to flowers
that I felt like saying goodbye.

At the hospital I admitted who I was
but names didn't matter.
I was a case straightaway.
A soft bracelet defined me.
It would see me right through,
I thought, to the crematorium.

I scrambled onto the trolley
as onto my bier.
I was almost blithe.
Half-gone, already laid out,
canula ready in my hand's blue vein
to drink down the end.

Why did I crawl back up
to the call of a name?
The worst of it has been
to wake to your face
wavering turnip moon
in the too-white ward.

Is this being alive?
As soon as my eyes could focus
I checked the trajectory
of yours. Your honey beam
fell on the pillow
just to your right of my head.

I am not that woman.
I am another, thin as a doily.
I'll give you the slip again.
I won't be around
for either you or cancer
to see your reflection.

The deep bone pain
after surgery reassures me.
My dear body is somewhere
near at hand. It's been
months away as your lover.
Now it's weeping for what it grew.

Keep looking. Keep looking.
Now I'm out of your sight
I'll put on my flesh again.
Pain is centering me
like wedged clay on the wheel.
It's a start.

Damson-Fall in the Study of Dove Cottage

for Dorothy Wordsworth

An unseen letting-go, as of budscales –
the narrow twigs sigh upwards, straighten,
callouse their circular and crescent scars

A shoal of dark fish in the shallows
stunned, wounds beaded with mites,
the grasses' undulant threads netting them close

Slack and damp to my hands
that comb them out – little minnows,
little plummeted lapwings

I have held them for seasons after,
their clear blood light in a glass,
their sharp preserve

but these walls hold them truest –
whitewash of blossom from their scrubbed spring
stained with the crush of their dying –

damson-fool.

The Second Home Delivery

It's like the last weeks of carrying a child –
all the stiff cartilage of the pelvis softening,
the ur-joints remembering themselves, the bone plates
open to undulation, open to opening.

Is it the house or me that's growing riper?
We belly together like two fresh figs, as slack
and silky. No angles in us now. Bone
of brick slithers into curves. Mortar's a lubricant.

House and I tenting to the wind's tempo,
catching air, not light. Hours, and now day and night
getting beyond us. Even this far inland
it's atlantic weather we move to

and the wind whipples the walls as if
we were canvas. I am cellaring down,
tracking my own clock at the almost
navel of England. How your absence

has uncorseted me! I have let ourselves go.
Shelves tip. All the knick-knacks and crockery,
the cutlery of all our lives, cascade –
a flash flood of the familiar.

For Tom

The ramparts of your face
are a steep pale citadel
from a Book of Hours: September.

Death has sharpened your verticals
and bleached them stone-white,
moved you to a middle distance

so that when I lean across
for a last brush of hand to forehead
I can only just reach you

across the chill plain of linen.
There's still yield to your skin.
It's not yet shrunk to fit

the bone of you, though all
that made it yours is gone
to lard and pucker. Most I miss

your rough cheeks' broken veins,
a tiny damage that we're told
is irreversible.

II

ACROSS THE WATER

Silk and Belfast Linen

I THE LAMPSHADE MAKERS

First, a slow and ravelled bandaging
of wire, the soldered junctions awkward,
the frame a snare for their wrists,
and that flat card of cross-cut binding
a footling shuttle as they lay the tape's
raw edge round ferrous metal
that would else, in this sporey climate, oxidise.

And then they take their trousseaux
all to bits – all their night things
snip-snipped to a panel pattern:
the camisoles and wedding negligées
of silk and silk-satin and silk-mousseline.
They cut away chafed seams, stained underarms,
faint foxing of blood below.

Oh, there are stretches that are good
as new, blush pink and peachy!
These they seam into a sleeve of silk
and raise a taut pavilion.
                              Now
silk's in eclipse until its lamp is lit.

II SHEARS

In the linen mills I was a weaver of linen.
(That was before I married Billy Morrow.)
My own loom, uh huh, my own web.
Them was great times. Forty of us girls
pedalling Belfast linen on forty looms.

But yer man – Robinson, was it? – would saunter along
the aisle of the looms. Didn't he have the quick eye
for a slub in the damask, even a thickened thread.
He had soft hands. The other checkers 'd point
so as you could mend it. Robinson? Oh no.

His wee white nail 'd
pick and pick and pick
till that slub was a hole in the web
and the pink prick of his finger
poked right through.

'Yon's a fault!' Robinson dandered his shears
handy like, at his belt. In four snips
he'd cut the warp in two. 'That'll larn ye.'

Mebbe a day's piece gone. Mebbe a week's.
Whatever it was, it was a ruin of linen.
Priceless. The girl wageless. And in debt for the yarn.

III PEGGING OUT

I was snapping the creases from damp linen
and damp cotton, making small bangs
of the sort the wind makes when it's hard
on the clothes, and they give off reports like a flag
or even a whip.
                    As I stretched one pillowcase
crack! it ripped in ten places
all parallel in a laddery sort of run:
the last of our wedding linen.

The frame of drawn threadwork's still intact,
that for twenty-five years was a dotted line
for no one to tear along.

It's the body that's given way, the holder of pillow,
worn by the rub of ears, abrasion of hair, by pillowtalk
and washing, washing, washing.
                        I thought
of my mother and father, still pulling and snapping
sheets between them after forty-nine years
and I laughed, laugh now at my freedom
out there in the silvery weather of the falling year.

The Women's Journey

From the stiff curd of the centre lands
    once a year
we slice off to the rim
leaving reducing cauldrons of the heart
    to simmer on.

We are unsure of bounds and marches
    straddling marks –
rare our treks
to such wet edges of the moon-ruled world
    such foreign parts . . .

       time outside time in the gappy suture
          of now to now,
       time dipped in fords
       and here made clear in laving of a sea.
          O glassy time!

       We lean on wind from ocean's vastness
          we are plucked
       and burnished by its air.
       From such translucency and marklessness
          we must return . . .

Ours is a burnt fertility inland
    a matter of
mutterings and sooty roofs.
Our menfolk hold displenishing sales of skulls
    mix ash with seed.

We find them scraping the scraw
    on our return.
The bonefires smoulder.
We cross our sills and swing the pots to cool
    on whitening hearths.

Lir: By His Sons

He was absent. Or we absented ourselves
from his large entrances, his enthronements
all flap and report of whip and papers.

If we could serve for him at those gatherings,
stretch up and between and over to dispense
morsels and liquids to his leaning peers . . . !

We pushed our sister first through the door's gape,
squealing a little, all of us, in the dark hallway.
Quieting quick as we stepped through into the blaze.

His wakings were fearsome. The track of his snores
fractured and swallowed itself, then he spewed
in a slew of leg from under the covers.

We ran for him, ran from him, as he uncloaked
his pig belly and his plucked-goose balls,
the purple of his cock's soft wattle.

Liadain to Cuirithir

I CHANGING ELEMENTS

The otter must enter his holt
                through water
water that's stilled and steady
well-deep to catch the print
of high-flying birds.

The otter with pale grey feet
must leave through water:
dry home, wet element
staking his life on margins.

                He'll shrug
small seeds of liquid, of air
from his preened pelt
seaming the two with light

will scatter the rayed fish
to a halo along the veins
of tributary streams.

I have watched from darkness
wishing for otter, alert
for the whistle, the splash of limbs.

II THE LAST TIME

In the sunken green-road
of our act of terminus
we beat the bounds.

It was no camping
on a honey-field
but hidden, bloody.

The sparse ash caught
as much of clouded blue
over our last holding

as I would keep
into the curt days
of the season of the dead.

Then I loosed you onto
the fluent seaways,
the ovals of the waves.

You left me be
skin to skin with ice
on the tundra of parting

your flagstone over my face.

Note: The ninth century Irish text *Liaidain and Cuirithir* tells of the love of Liaidain, a poet from Munster, and Cuirithir, a poet from Connaught. Cuirithir's name means 'otter's son'.

By Lough Swilly – 1609/1959

It is a drought summer. In the fields
cropmarks   postholes   earthworks   reappear.

The mud and sandflats of the estuary
bloom with purple like a heated iron.

In a hollow of the trickling dunes
the man is painting. No one will believe
he saw such gaudy, he whose palette is
all leached and pastel, water caught in oils.

The woman watches. Standing on the quay –
Rathmullen, where the great earls once embarked
for Normandy, then to their graves in Rome –
she feels their anguish across centuries.

The Feast of the Exaltation of the Cross
it was, that harvest day that they departed.
'Walk while ye have the light, lest darkness come
upon ye, for he that walketh in the dark
knoweth not whither he goeth.' And Ulster grieved
and moved in darkness, all her counsel spent.

Even in heat like this their failure chills.
Nuala, Cathbar, the son not one year old,
the countess Catherine with her three young boys,
Tyrone, Tyrconnell – these are what she sees
upon the glittering channels of the lough,
this sun a monstrance for the dispossessed.

Epithalamion for Midsummer Day,
Gleann da Locha

Last night the bonefires spoke
to the sun, calling its gold
down onto corn set green.

Today there has been no let
to the rain that spills and rivers
staining the ash with dark.

By evening there'll be a gush
will build its humming spate
to a force, a waterfall

and we'll roll our pleasures down
the tumble of filmy hills
in the long midsummer dusk.

    Tonight on our first hearth
    I will smoor the fire
    this night and every night
    each single night

Calling on Annie at Holly Hill

The parlour's cold in a heatwave. She has logs
well-caught and flamey for us. But our backs!
The beech trees sieve the wind like sea through shingle.

She is shaking for Jimmy, dead now nearly a year.
Dead two days when they found him, in the old caravan
across the yard from the house that has fallen to ruin.

Ten in the morning, and her hand shakes as she pours
from cut glass to cut glass. Such grief for a brother.
Do I ever want to love a man so much

that his death would give my limbs a tremor like hers?
One that the years won't settle?
And is it because you are still walking this earth

that I'm firm on my feet? That I don't shake for you?

Mare Crisium

Over the warrenkeeper's fallen hearth
a growing moon, clear enough to show
the shadows of its own highlands cast
upon itself, and that great northern range
pulling a clue of light out across darkness
to the unlit *Sinus Iridum.*

                In Gweebarra Bay
the tide's most reach has laid the red of dulse
high on the shell-sand, a smear of knowable dead,
vegetable, animal. Offshore the wintering loon
rolls and preens, a manifest of white
against the salt Atlantic.

                The swallowed ebb
rests somewhere under where the bird might drift,
a phase of moon and moment, markless, immersed.
And at what turning did the hazel root
its rod of patched silver through bramble pioneers,
raise slabs from true?

On the Slopes of Croagh Patrick

The air a given –
and measure of views
wholly in its gift –

this mercury rim to the sea
skids into distance
under pressing cloud.

Mountain behind us is
mere fierceness of green
at its grazed root

screeslopes and ling-scrub
lost, like all sky seaward
and over us,

to the one great vapour
of the coming storm.

From land's low glow
off to the shone horizon
air gives a tarnished silver
to the sea

                gives whale-shape
to the drowned moraines
that island Clew Bay.

We are breathing that pressed air
within the spirit
of the sea's bright level

at this last centre of light
are cuffed by winds
rising to squall-force –

gale that will have blown
by morning a glassy sphere
for tomorrow's measure.

Holly-Fall, Maghera

I TINNE

I hold my hollyn bobbe
into the silver waning of the year.

The leaves I've cast
are chamois and dawn light.
My bark is map-lichen
regions of the moon.

The leaves I hold
tense their wire against winter
their slung leather shiny
as apples, dark as yew.

II TIP

From evergreen I watch
deciduous metals:

Car door that creaks and creaks
in the stone gap.
The wire loop hinges, the wire
that hoops it closed.

Bracts of rust. A bed
that's fallen the wrong side
out of a room.
Scattered gifting of ring-pulls.

III CRIB

The wayside shrine is green
with a piece of me

its fallen pane on the grass
like a puddle's ice lid, lifted
and sliced by the diamond
waves of shock.

Only a short drop, surely,
from that chill crib
to this rimmed, obtuse
trigonometry?

IV 1658

Under Slievetooey I am
least forest on a shadowed hill

chinewood, shaftwood
grown slow on quartzite
facing north over sea
to a land of green rushes O

*and oh for the child
with her taper of rushlight
when the soldiers looked south
and saw gleams on Slievetooey*

*and oh for the people
who thought themselves hidden
in the cave of my roots
when the slaughter began.*

V CAMBIUM

I go all ways under light

swallow the solstice
down my straight limbs
down to the root.

A hall of mirrors,
the cells within me
proliferate light

white glow that only
a kerf to the quick
will spill into air.

My bright blood
blinks on the snow
beaded and berried.

Let-Down

for Medbh McGuckian

When my milk came in, oh not *my* milk, the child's –
well whose? can I say clearly? though I did
taste it once, a thin hazelnut water –
well, when it came in, it stood blue-veined in my breasts
and I could not express it. My breasts were as hard to grip
as Hallowe'en apples, the ones you hang on strings
from a clothes airer hauled to the ceiling, and try to bite.
Oh my breasts were hard as Bramleys
and my nipples tender as a cut.
The child could not catch on. How would she, the scrap?
And she wept, and the other babies around me wept
for the milk I had and to spare, but could not express.

When I no longer could lay my arms by my sides
and the midwife was threatening a drug to suppress lactation
it came to me, the dark shed in Rathmullen
and the child I was that summer, pressing all
the left side and ear of her head against
the leathern flank of the cow, pulling, learning
the rhythm, the teat music
as the milk jet jangled onto galvanised metal
or drove richly into the foam of itself.
That double note. The sound of relief.
The nee-naw rhythm of rescue.

The child that was me couldn't, of course, get the hang.
But the mother I suddenly am hears the pitch of percussion
deepen as the bucket fills, its long diminuendo . . .
My shirt front's wringing, and when I unfasten my bra
two jets of milk rise in two crossing arcs
right over the head of my nuzzling wavery child.

III

TURAS

Aran of the Saints

I have come over water, my arms
sleeved in companionable sea
that pleats in muslin from the hull.

I have met your mouth as it parts
for ocean and me to enter.

The soles of my feet are blistered
from walking the hard stations:

    Birmingham, Holyhead,
    the streets of Galway City.

I have walked the rounds of waiting.

Pattern Day

Inisheer, the smallest of the Aran Islands, has a number of ancient settlements and churches buried under its shifting sands. The seventh century church of Saint Cavan in the island burial ground is dug out each summer for Mass to be said on his feast – or pattern – day in mid-June.

I

The graveyard is a mounting dune of sand.
Slipping a rosary of bones it climbs
within the ruined chapel's pace-thick walls.

In its soft flour of shells the island souls
still hunkered on their resurrection ground
await the living and the not long dead.

They sense the year's slow breathing out to full –
soon men will strip the fetch of winter storms
from Cavan's church, will lay its pattern bare.

II

Long-shafted shovels lean on masonry
damp and salted from a year's blown sand.

Men have filled creel and creel, and pinned the dune
back to itself with wooden stay-stitching

and here they build a sanctuary of air
find the moist nave, strike heart-blades on old flags

as slowly they lower Cavan's church to light.

III THE CHURCH SPEAKS

Sun mounts to solstice,
sand is creeled away –
my pattern's made.

I am harled of turf's enamel
trefoil and heartsease
and the fine dune grass.

I am dressed down to stone
to host the feast.

Dry, dry, as salt tightens
whiteness on cracked lime.

Sun rasps unmortared joints
wedges his noontime bulk
into my hold.

Pulled plants wither
parched haulm splits with drought.

My eastern windhole
is blanked out with sand.

No light onto pale hills
of distant Connaught
nor onto sea

only its bitter taste
on my altar's cloth of slate

only the notched cross
shrunk out of true.

IV IUBE ME VENIRE AD TE SUPER AQUAS

Then the pilgrims come
sail west to the summer solstice.
White midnights are about them.
God's elbow has buffed the sea
to an opal shine that's fretted
with currents, tides, the plucking
of June's finicky winds.

About them gannets hurl
great bolts into shoals of fry,
auks glean in the furrows.

Leaving the solid uplands,
the hazel thickets, behind them
they have cast themselves on the waters.
Saint Cavan hauls them in
on a silver spinner of light.
Small surf lifts them to sandfall.
They step from the green to the white.

V THE VIGIL AT THE SAINT'S BED

Murmur of vigil in this sounding-hole –
the brief night's rubbed away
in beads of prayer.
In His hands' cool shadow
He has hidden me.
Out over Inishmaan
hangs the first star.

Pilgrims kneel on fading turf that nets
midden of shells, bones
in their shifting yard.
One man leans
hugging the gravehead cross
of one he loves
black against bluer dark.

Another will not settle to kneel or lean.
His son, one of the Lebanon's disappeared,
has no grave he knows.
This woman bleeds, bleeds
and cannot conceive.
That one prays for the mother
she soon must lose.

Ailing or broken they would be made whole
of griefs that riddle
from their moving lips.
Here shall their cares be knit
their sores annealed
for this holy now
in midnight's velvet nap.

The Bed of Cavan holds a steady air
for slipping candles –
a butter-meadow of flame.
    This vigil is sleep.
    This healing is women and men
    laying an ear to grass
    slow lung to stone.

What will they take when stone and air and distance
startle from night
and an orange zest of moon
    swings up in the east?
    when pipits and grounded larks
    mutter and flute
    and the time of vigil is gone?

What will they take down to their sheeted beds
in the unlit houses
when candle-ends gutter to dawn?
    A thin ravel of sand
    will start to reclaim
    Cavan's swept slab
    as a new losing's begun.

Note: The son lost in the Lebanon was a member of the UN peacekeeping troops whilst serving in the Irish army.

VI THE CHURCH SPEAKS

It is noon of this day.
Wind matches the sun
blow for smart blow.
I lie under it, scoured
to a structure of silence
salt in my mouth, bleached.

Come with white linen
and the pale sea-stock.
My slate is clear.
Set on it book
and candles globed against the wind,
bright cup, bright plate.
Come with your warm flesh
under my roof of air.
Make a meal in me.

Scatter of coolness as rain
starts out of sunlight
out of untraceable cloud –
slow drops that ring and fade
on my sucking stones
fierce for the easing
of their tongues' dry root.

Now cloud cuts out
colour's transparency,
rain is a moving skin.
I am glossed and deepened.
Drink this, as I do.
Take into drought
this overcast, this dark.

VII THE PILGRIM LOOKS BACK
FROM THE MAINLAND OF CONNEMARA

You lie in the south quarter.
I wake with you in my eye
across the channel's sheet.

Currents ruck colour into
pale and pale between us.
This is the lull of dawn.

I search the dark cleft
of your only valley's spring.
I cannot see its green

nor the mound of sand that falls
always into the kist
of bone and memory –

only your blown heart
held above darkening sea
where all is beached.

Mending

I

He resets the stones of a wall
that the wind or a passing housecow
tumbled, his knuckles bloodied
by limestone's weathered edge.

'The Church of the Seven Daughters?
You're near enough upon it
hid in its brake of briars.'

II

I walk between stone walls
so high they shut out sight
of pasture, distant sea,
of all but the paling ranks
of further enclosing walls.
Saint Ignatius, I almost
do your spiritual workout,
my straying eyes contained.
Getting nearer, released
from straitness by a stile
onto hardbitten grazing
I try to meditate
a tumbled faith into being,
gaze on incised stone.

III

'And did you find it?' he asks.
' 'Tis grand, though few that visit
have patience to seek it out.

'This island is full of the graves
of saints, and of the people
were here before Christ's word.

'No man of Inisheer
would lay his hand to shift
a slab or header from them.'

He beds a through-stone with
a peg of smaller rock,
straightens from his task.

'We have a past that is
hunger, too. We know
the body's crying out.

'And so we raise a tithe –
this year for the starving poor
of Nicaragua.

'May God have pity on Reagan.'

IV

The rock in ocean sharpens
with slant sun from the west.
A snipe is flushed from the bank
where the generator chirrs
and house after house tunes in
to television, the viewing
of what is far away.

Note: Ronald Reagan visited Galway City during its quincentenary celebrations
in 1984.

Sandshift: Aranmor to Inisheer

The western island has sent of its great strand,
stripped flag-cell and field wall
clear to the marram spit.
Shaped stone gapes at the light.

Fragmentary earth is a mist
that holds against blue,
for the wind is passing its grain
through the high gut of the air.

A column of unfused glass
tools over sea and the slight
sand-dollar islands,
losing and rising, losing.

On the eastern island
what is kept from the waters comes
as a white glasspaper hail-fall
that dredges all skin with sharpness.

The island mothers are shawling their children
in gritty blankets to school.
The loaded wind is biting
the tender backs of their knees.

The lashes of men and animals
mesh, the molluscs are shuttered.
Soft and vegetable parts
are scored with the travel of salt.

Only inanimate land
can meal it at last to stillness
and softness now on the stones
it whitens back into dark.

Saint Gobnaít, Leaving Inisheer

A blether of chanting bees on honey sward
about my skep of stone, round cell of silence –
wild angelica, hartstongue that thirsts for streams,
cranesbill shiny and bloody like my Lord.

The long blue bird leans on the topmost course
of wall after wall, chiding the cuckoo farmer
late in sowing, slow in the raking of kelp.
Its soft and solitary yelling urges 'to sea'

that I must pass over again before I find
the cold and stony place of my resurrection.

One flitting would do me all my days of life.
Here is my hive's bole, this cleft in the rock.
Must I plait grey marram, bind it with split briar
to make once more a travelling box for my bees?

Seething ciborium stopped with balsam, adrift
and angry, sapping its inner store of sweets –
I whisper to them of death as we pass the surf
swing onto ridge and furrow of forageless sea.

I have rubbed their empty house with bedstraw flowers
to summon a wild swarm. My door swings in the wind.

Note: Saint Gobnaít is the patron saint of Irish beekeepers. A vision called her
away from her chosen sanctuary in the island of Inisheer, and back to the
mainland of Ireland. She later founded a monastery in Co. Cork.

Islands

INISBOFFIN

Island of the White Cow
follows my creases like the moon
over the dunes smoked white
by a big blow –

                                    cow
creamy as mooncarrot
or her own frothed milk
haunched with plump and hollow
in the meadowsweet foam of the sea.

TORY ISLAND

Moonless night
and the coast not clear.
Tory, grey as the pig-iron sea
it is raised from –
the cut wards of a key
the straight Yale stock of it
set on a rim of sea-light.
Its outcrops yield nothing
but tar-lichen's
oxide stain.

ON HOLY ISLAND

On the dry salt rocks
the green cross of a cormorant

the plumes of its body
a vest of stranded moss

the gloss of its bent wings
lapped in fringed bracts

to a wide calyx
for stilled muscles of flight

its pinions green as ash
or crucifer leaves.

It is laid out
in the white shadow of frost

over basalt holding the cold
of long slow winter.

The green sound swells
lower than whelk-line

lower than the black seam
where worms will root

after the thaw.

INISKEEL: WINTER

A new moon, and last night
a gale from the north and west.
Kelp from the lower shore –
frond, stipe and holdfast
driven in tangles.
Sea at our door.
                    Rooks
in the gold air of morning
pick in the brass salt weed.

Island of the lost bell
the moon and the wind are your arbiters.
These are the days when you are
all island, the strand of a way to you
wished for from water and light,
the under-over of waves that cross each other,
angular mesh of sea. Unwadable.
We cannot imagine an ebb that will take
that step – backwards, downwards, away.

The Greening of China

I

I had no companion on the road.
The brown silt lifted and blew
into the channels
that keep green from green.

My journey sloped and lifted
not as the silt, but rather
as a saucer in section
or a moon that's hollow-ground.

So many gravity rhythms
in that dip and scoop –
the balletic poise
of telegraph wires, of tides.

II

Dry stubble in the fishponds.
I knew milky spring
would flood the valley
for the grass-carps' grazing.

On Piled Silk Hill
a floating shelf of rock
would step me over
the jade waters and cloud.

Green distances would yield
the outcrops of the world
like beacon summits
lighting a story home.